THE FLAWS

IN THE STORY

The Flaws in the Story

LIANE STRAUSS

MARSH HAWK PRESS · 2024

East Rockaway, New York

MARSH HAWK PRESS • 2024

East Rockaway, New York

Copyright © 2024, Liane Strauss

Marsh Hawk books are published by Marsh Hawk Press, Inc.,
a not-for-profit corporation under section 501(c)3
United States Internal Revenue Code.

Cover art: Edouard Vuillard. *Album Cover for Landscapes and Interiors*, 1899.
The Art Institute of Chicago.
Cover and interior design & typesetting: Mark Melnick

FIRST EDITION

Library of Congress Cataloging-in-Publication Data
Names: Strauss, Liane, author.
Title: The flaws in the story / by Liane Strauss.
Description: First edition. | East Rockaway, New York : Marsh Hawk Press, 2024.
Identifiers: LCCN 2023033647 | ISBN 9780998658278 (paperback)
Subjects: LCGFT: Poetry.
Classification: LCC PS3619.T74345 F56 2024 | DDC 811/.6--dc23/eng/20230721
LC record available at https://lccn.loc.gov/2023033647

Marsh Hawk Press, Inc.
P.O. Box 206, East Rockaway, N.Y. 11518-0206
mheditor@marshhawkpress.org

for Jim

Contents

To all she offers hopes, and has promises for each man, sending them messages,
but her mind is set on other things. And she devised in her heart this guileful
thing also: she set up in her halls a great web, and fell to weaving—fine of
thread was the web and very wide; and straightway she spoke among us: 'Young
men, my wooers, since goodly Odysseus is dead, be patient, though eager for my
marriage, until I finish this robe—I would not that my spinning should come
to naught—a shroud for the lord Laertes, against the time when the fell fate
of grievous death shall strike him down; lest any of the Achaean women in the
land should be wroth with me, if he, who had won great possessions, were to
lie without a shroud.' So she spoke, and our proud hearts consented. Then day
by day she would weave at the great web, but by night would unravel it. . . .

—Homer, *Odyssey*, Book II

I

Sugar

It was the night you were telling me your idea for a movie, the first Yom
Kippur after my father died. Lila and I

had stayed up late, talking about her mother, the selfless narcissist. That's what
my brother calls her, Lila said.

Also: The woman who is a cross between an echo and an abyss. An
undeveloped character

in an abandoned text by Beckett. The thing that cannot stop circling back.
Which always makes me think of a doubt

or a vulture, and the way she picks at the liver of her own sacred litany of
lifelong sacrifices, pulling on them

like the broken levers of an obstinate machine, pulling them on like a
lamentable pair of ancient donkey socks,

her cold toes poking through the disappointing threads like the hopeless
loophole Thomas's gutsy digits discovered.

And after all I've done, she fumily sputters, winding up in apparent disgust,
this is the thanks I get. Lila

is a theoretical mathematician when it comes to her mother. Any way you
divide her, she likes to say, Mother conquers

and remains less than the sum of her parts. And yet no matter how many times
she has repacked and fastened her own suitcases

for the last time, Lila can't subtract herself from that irrational equation.
There was something in this

of the way I couldn't seem to shake the image of Jacob Bronowski wading out
knee-deep into the muddy river

near Auschwitz. It was the way he was standing in it as he scooped up a
handful of that trickling mud

made with the DNA of his murdered family. That's what had come back to
haunt me. The way it spilled back out

from between his fingers. The way he seemed to be trying to turn anger into
philosophy. Something

about it chimed with your story, the sight of your boss weeping at his own
announcement

of your imminent departure, how it led us to wonder if that was what it was
like to be a landowner at the end of serfdom,

and together we watched the long line of scarified pans leaping and bouncing
silently against the impotent flanks

as the freshly liberated led the last of their shabby mules down the rutted track
and into the sunset of the middle class—

Well, that was the dream.

Every article that week had been fueled by the rage against sugar and the new
sex drug,

only the latest incarnation of the long line of better things by Dupont. Truly
    there was no way around the evidence

to indicate that the more we know, the less we are inclined to think about
    anything. I for one, in spite of having read my Lucretius

had yet to get the hang of understanding dreams qua dreams, my own or
    anyone else's, convinced that I could

see right through them all the way into the kitchen behind the counter in the
    big new Levain Bakery window.

But now, suddenly, at this late hour, it was starting at last to be clearer and
    clearer that whether it was what we set our sights on,

or what we were moving every day steadily and farther away from, there was
    less and less evidence to suggest

we would someday get our hands on what was missing. Although there was
    still hope. There was always hope

Listen More, Talk Less

That was the advice she wanted to give to the daughter of her friend, she said.

It's the advice I wish someone had given me at that age, the advice I would give myself if I could go back and—

and listen. I couldn't resist.

It was the day after tax day and the insistent wind that had stormed the town, howling and whistling

and tormenting the windows up and down the avenues like the pack of wolves bedeviling the caribou on Our Planet.

I had watched that episode with the children before bed and I didn't know whether that was what woke them

or the storm, louder than the avalanching crashes of the spears of ice eighty stories high and the stacks of snow

so dense and white they were blue and looked like meringues just when they get that creamy sheen and you're supposed to stop beating them

sheering off the heights all night and roiling the waters off of Greenland,

and this morning Notre Dame like the Twin Towers on the cover of all the
    papers,

but there was no switching her off her track, not a chance of derailing her.

She blinked once, like an owl thinking about a mouse

and barreled on, past the models of commuters artfully positioned on all the
    local platforms.

Think of all the trouble I could save her!

But all I could think of were the parents going to jail for sending their children
    to the ivy leagues (why did that make me think of the gulag)

and who was going to save them

and the krill that live off the algae that live in the ice

and how food chains are a kind of chain, but one that shouldn't be broken,

while there are others that are more like Blake's manacles, or chain reactions,
    nuclear, and harder to break,

which reminded me of "The Charge of the Light Brigade," doomed, as
    Tennyson understood, from the beginning.

All the endless analysis is good, as you like to say, but where does it get you.

I wanted to say something when I saw her over spring break, she was saying.

I was half-listening, half-wondering whether it was something to do with the
    intersection of linguistics and biology,

the way the shape of our words fails to fit with the shape of our ears, perhaps,
    that makes us incapable of hearing

anything said directly, as the crow flies,

an expression which means we know it's impossible,

or the way track is laid, along parallel lines,

and whether they used to fit better, like maybe when we spoke Sumerian

and there's been some kind of degradation alongside the evolution that so
many people assume is progress,

or whether it's just communication's natural proclivity toward all forms of
deception, the way we hedge our emotional but not just our emotional bets,

the way some forms of survival are flatly self-destructive,

and whether humans are the only ones for whom that is true, and if only we
were better at making use of it.

I keep remembering the time my late husband threw the Scrabble board across
the bedroom, she was saying,

how for weeks afterwards I kept coming across those unlikely tiles in the
craziest of places,

a Q deep in a corner in the pocket of my bathrobe, an E nestled on the edge of
the windowsill.

There was even a poor little W that had landed somehow in the dust and folds
of the curtains

I only found years later, on the phone with my mother

telling me again how nothing I ever did surprised her

Baudrillard's Widow

It must have been what Dewey calls *the forces*. And here's me having always
    since I guess the third grade thought

of him as more or less synonymous with decimals and libraries and systems.
    But, *Ach du lieber*, as my Bavarian grandfather liked to say,

if this isn't a different Dewey altogether. The decimals in my eyes were
    pounding and panting and stinging the way they used to

in school, even after I turned down the lights and lay in my bed and closed the
    stacks to fall right back into Kafka's labyrinth

of ladders and high grids and spines—that grand illusion of order, like
    Haussmann's Paris, and had I really never noticed

the logic and irony of his Teutonic name, this was my paradoxical thought as I
    picked my way through blades of dust

and light stray chinks flung into gullies through the windowless wilderness
    onward back toward the conversation

that had wormed its hungry tunnel all the way to Baudrillard's widow, her
    view, to be precise, of what keeps men

over eighty happy. But, although I've never been sure how this is possible, I
  seem to be getting ahead of myself

and what I don't want to do most of all is leave out the woman we thought we
  recognized, the tall one

with red hair and the beautiful voice, from Arkansas, with whom I ended up
  posing for a photo as if we were

long-lost, serendipitously reunited relations in Balthazar's on a finally
  summery evening before

sitting back down, where the forces—I don't believe there is a better name for
  them—were systematically at work

within or behind or maybe underneath the conversation, which, like any
  conversation, is just a surface, isn't it, or a lid

that can't keep things in or back or down. Or out, for that matter. And which
  gets broken, as in by Bonnard's wife's kneecaps,

or her chin, in the purples of his vision of her bath, which always looks, to me
  anyway, like yet another early twentieth-century

watery death, cue *The Waste Land*. They say he was dedicated to her, Bonnard.
  Like a book, maybe. Or, in his way.

And maybe hers, too. After all, hadn't I just the week before sat next to the
  breathless gentleman from Yorkshire

whose parents had packed him off, along with his twin brother, to the bookish
  Benedictines at the age of eight?

He adored his American wife of very nearly thirty years now, as he hastened to
assure me, and I had no cause

to doubt his word before he broached the subject of the one thing they'd never
seen eye to eye on. That was the day

before the day in the Pocket Bar on Forty-eighth where you and I rolled our
eyes at the TA who assured your Lucie

that one thing they could not talk about was Shakespeare's intentions, since
we could never know them. Well, I said,

if the unknowable is off-limits, what next? But you weren't having any. As if
she knew her own better than we might,

speculating here in a bar in a pocket of Forty-eighth Street. I suppose it's one
thing to be hoist on your own

good intentions, you continued, trailing off, and I pointed to the jungle in the
Rousseau someone had written

the menu over, loosing animals among the decimals. So you will understand
how it was that evening

that my eyes growled and lowed, even though it was the left, the farseeing one,
more than the right,

which is the one I read with. How it must have been from watching the lid
tremble and sputter like an expression

of Euler's definition of the gamma function calculating factorials of the
fractions animating that evening's

forces. And how, hours later, far from Rousseau's Arkansas, Old Testament
   riddles, Shakespeare's Paris,

Kafka's Yorkshire terrier, Baudelaire's swan's petard and the mad leaps and
   dashes of Dewey's reckless promises

I closed my aching eyes, like a book whose text had turned to water, to climb
   into my once familiar dark and marvel

at the power of boats over the male octogenarian and the beautiful intelligence
   it seemed to contain within it

I Need To Learn
To Lie Better

My grandmother was the Barnum and Bailey of liars. I could hear her shaking
   her head after I told Frederick

what I really thought about his grandmother who had waited thirteen lucky
   years for her guerrilla fiancé,

his grandfather, while he was hiding out in the jungle, coming dangerously
   close to the catastrophe of her own spinsterhood.

She must have had some idea what he would have done to her if she hadn't. I
   still say he ought to have known better

since I had already shown my hand when he told us about his uncle driving
   backwards through the Amazon

for seven hours. At night. He had just learned, Frederick told us, that my aunt,
   his fiancée, was ill, and his car

was stuck in reverse. But when he got there it turned out she had nothing more
   than a head cold. That reminds me

of the one about the car trying to back out of the multistory garage: There's an
   exit, the attendant shouted

pointing to the signs. I know, the car cried back, but that's not the same thing!
    If you are facing the ocean,

my grand equivocator of a grandmother once told me—we were on our way to
    San Francisco together

in the early years of her widowhood and she was contemplating the frozen sea
    of silent clouds out her window like an aerialist

gauging her leap into the arms of the approaching trapezist—the waves can't
    knock you down you while you're not looking.

If you don't want to be knocked down by the big waves, I reasoned, you can
    just step back up onto dry land.

Ah, she said, you were always too smart for me, and she squeezed my hand in
    the way that meant I was her favorite

The Secret

1.

The air was thick and heavy, a tongue drunk on a bee bite. My thoughts lay in the soft fist of a bud,

which meant I needed to protect them. How? From what? What had I missed? (What had I seen?) The dew

still clinging. Black lilies. None of it yet ready to speak or be spoken. Like proving. In a presentable. Greaves laced up.

And there he was, Achilles, holed up in his tent like an adolescent, suckling his grievance, but not (yet)

grieving. And yet sulking is a form of grieving. Grieving unformed. A form of grief foreshadowed, as adolescence

foreshadows the forms its wards are destined to grow into, and shields them from the knowledge of it. As unformed thoughts

presage speech and must be shielded from the shaft of words that by some fluke may find the heel and halt the bloom

and land you in a different flowerbed altogether. Nipped, as we say, in the bud. Silence, therefore. Silence and time.

And here at last lay the first real funereal bloom, an irony of a peace with my
   unfinished imagery

2.

It was 2017, and the learned half-cousin of the deceased had read from
   Exodus, aptly enough, speaking after his wife

and children. For we are not, she had said, only those standing here today, but
   also those who are not

here. It was obvious, but also mysterious, in the manner of the best puzzles.
   Like the life of the man

whom I had hardly known, in fact, from Moses, and from whose funeral I was
   walking home this sidelong

morning, alone, in a city of millions, apart from the muted, lingering, stifling,
   philosophical thunderstorms

of the night before, fuller of rumination than Sturm und Drang, and maybe
   too the ones to come, threatening,

the sun behind the clouds pressing on the clouds like a small boy on a heavy
   door

3.

Empty, the plangent streets were now, so the chapel had been filled, peopled,
   to every last seat, mourners

lining the walls like an art collection or a library turned hall of empty mirrors
   suddenly, without a face

to reflect them back to themselves. What of the unacknowledged mourners?
The ones who were not there,

who had slipped into their places as if no one in the legerdemain of funerals
would notice. There

and not there, like the man at the end of my row, leaning against the wall in a
sealskin coat. He had had

to blow his nose twice, his handkerchief fluttering like the fluted corolla of a
lily, while he rested against

the closed black lily of his umbrella

4.

There are always secrets. Of course there are. Everyone had them. There had to
be secrets. Like Margarét.

Who in God's green earth was Margarét? And certainly the man they were
driving, while I walked home,

to his grave in the rain had had his fill. A lifetime's worth, a whole secret life
alongside the other one.

What would we call it? The *visible* one? No, secrets are visible. People, like
paintings and books,

can't help themselves. As if we were ourselves the water glass in the mirror our
own bewildered hands keep

reaching for and somehow missing. Known? No, secrets are known. There is
no secret that is not known

to a whole world, the way untold stories are also stories, though stories lived
   out elsewhere perhaps.

Lived and unlived. Like the difference between Achilles in his tent and
   Margarét weeping

for the golden grove she'd leave filled with all her unlived lives as well as for the
   one she'd live and have

to leave behind. And how do we choose? Do we love our unlived lives more,
   precisely because we didn't

love them, or was it ourselves, enough? Is that why we bury them, dead or
   alive, between the lines and in

the lines and behind the lines? Is this what poetry does, give us an obvious
   puzzle we can solve

in the face of a greater one, death always hiding behind its back while it points,
   in the form of deceptively straight

lines, to a world brimming with life? Lines like

5.

the serried ranks we made up, those of us who had filled a chapel to the rafters
   that morning to mourn

a man like Hopkins' Margarét and, indeed, Homer's Achilles, in another final,
   finite tribute to our own infinite,

Odyssean resourcefulness? For weren't we always finding new ways to
   stonewall and reveal ourselves, we

who are not only the self-evident, mysterious puzzles we can't solve, but also,
   like the impatient Thetis

rushing to keep her child safe from his fate, fated ever after herself to weigh in
   the book of her own hands

regret against regret, having chosen to hold onto him there, and not there

Tarzan
& Proust

The world is hard to love, and maybe that's what makes it lovable, like difficult
children, and ornery old men. It's not

the ones who all your life you think you're finally about to be able to avoid
because, finally, you see them coming

from a speck, as it were, to a specter. They always have another old surprise in
store, still manage to cast their best pall

across your clearest path and what promised to be an all but perfectly pleasant
afternoon. Maybe, you think, with enough

therapy you'll, finally, outgrow your susceptibility to them, like shellfish or
hurricanes

on the weather channel that look like the big one and keep sneaking into your
soup.

My mother would say it's because they haven't got enough to do. And,
paradoxically, maybe

if they found themselves more at loose ends. But when did words and phrases
ever represent the state of affairs they were said to be

representing? Recognizing which would have made it more difficult for my
father to keep reminding me this was

my journey. Instead, here's someone who needs to apologize. And here's
another who has never so much as tried

to so much as pretend, or vice versa, to minister unto anything suddenly
undertaking to instruct

me in the proper care of bougainvillea!

While I am trying to remember the first time I saw bougainvilleas, which was
in Proust, these two

are mobilizing compliments like an infantry of mercenaries to lavish me with
the vacuum of their attentions until

I am alone on an airstrip afraid to look up. How long will it be until I stop
flinching at every distant mower?

How much longer still until I move again in villas and in leas and, finally, am
able to recall

the second time, in Italy, when I turned a corner down a lane and came upon
the word made flesh, exclaiming, Bougainvillea!

to no one. To myself. Without stopping to think, as if I were myself the creator
and this word-made flesh

my idea. All of it. From cool green waves of leaves cascading down summer
walls to golden heartbeats flush

with coral, pink, persimmon, and that Rinascimento purple that almost hurts,
and all of it called

Bougainvillea!

because of me reaching for Proust, a lifeline like a vine dangling through the
canopy from which at any moment

I could escape all earthbound dangers and swing from one to the next, like
Jane on television all those year ago

North American Tree Frogs

*I was happy till I and Rachel were asked to spend three days at Colesborne,
to see Mr Elwes' butterflies, a thing I had much desire to do. . . . Mr Elwes'
wonderful collection making one thoroughly unsettled and discontented, I was
dissatisfied with my own collection in a way that was almost childish. 'Now you
see the possibilities of a collection,' Mr Elwes had said one day in the museum,
to which I had replied, that on the contrary I only saw the impossibilities . . . !*

FROM THE DIARIES OF MARGARET FOUNTAINE

It was nearly Thanksgiving, the first year of the global pandemic, yet wasn't it
   enough just to say

pandemic, like William Carlos Williams, and be done with it? If only it were
   that simple,

which begs the question, Was it ever? And, if so, when? Even though that's not
   what *begs the question*

means. Which begs the question, At just what point does the common or
   general understanding tip the balance? And,

What exactly are the holdouts holding out for? And, If we understand
   incorrectly, what are we understanding?

And, Why is it so deceptively hard to fathom that beauty is what lies

just beyond all our efforts to pin it down, like the Painted Lady in the garden,
and that Death is not

what the specimens pinned to the cloth in their cases knowingly exemplify.

Although we feel it, don't we, *underneath* the beauty, the way we feel the pin,
perhaps, for a moment, in passing,

that is, we imagine we do. And isn't this what the imagination is for? To feel
our way past the labels and the glass *into*

something we would only otherwise stand coldly peering into—

like a coal mine, or an icebox, or the life

of an *intrepid lady lepidopterist*—in order to bring something back?

But this poem isn't about butterflies, it's about tree frogs, because we had both
been taken by surprise on the long walk

through the deep woods at Middleton Place, darkness falling, as they say, but
rising too, arriving from all quarters, at how long

it had been since we had heard the sound of frogs of any description. There
weren't perhaps

too many of them, since, once we had identified the initial slow volley, we
listened for them more

than we heard. And whether it was because we listened so hard, hoping against
hope for the next throaty cry

as if they were lost and we were the search party sent to save them, or that it
was like being haunted by the living

having spent the afternoon conversing among the dead, we didn't want to
leave until we had heard the next one.

Just once more. Although eventually we had to.

And back in the car heading to Charleston, the airwaves once again full of the
pandemic

and the outgoing president, we considered how long we might have stayed
listening in the dark

and how the longer we did, the more it seemed, like all extreme cases, just a
microscopic look at who we always were

or should be, responsible for others as much as for ourselves, since from a
certain perspective there was

no difference, and how what was impossible was also what was wanted most of
all, and what it meant

that starting over was just a phrase and another way of saying doing it again,
since we sometimes seem to forget

every morning, every minute, it sometimes seems, all our most fervent
resolutions, as if they disintegrate

as the sound of the words hits the air and, if we don't stay to listen until we
hear them again, somehow

we lose what it was we were meant to save, and yet wasn't it amazing how tree
frogs each have their own way

of saying just what it is they were born to say, and how often they need to
repeat it

II

The Leonids

You tell me they are out there. I shut my eyes. I'm not trying to be difficult. It's genuinely hard for me to imagine.

We all have our limit, I suppose, and maybe here, in the red desert of Cormac McCarthy country, is mine.

I'm fine, I write in the rose-tinted dust of the windshield, adding the latest to my tally.

A dozen and one falls. We start the hard ride home.

It's the return that turns and burns you up.

The toll for the downhill thrill of accelerating out of the gate.

Is that what they're afraid of? Because I can tell them, Sure it hurts, but we all survive. The bruises the bucking

and shuddering leave behind subside, the screaming brakes fade. The bright cuts and shocks the salvo

of sharp sparks scatters last, I suppose. But unscathed is unchanged. And on that hopeful note I look up

from the dust where it was all writ clear.

You're smiling, but you're shaking your head. My hopeless hopefulness.

They're not even tempted? Never even attempt it? Your eyes widen silently.

But everyone wants to go there.

No, you say. No, not everyone. There are some, many, who can't see the point.

I consider the terrifying, testifying beauty of what you say they can't see, those
some, those many

but I'm the one scouring the dark now. What else is there? They can't be happy
to remain

here. I don't have to look up into your face to see I'm not getting it. I try again.
But even if they can't

see it they can *imagine*—You shake your head again. That's what they can't do.

This is where I get stuck, literally stuck, and suddenly I'm the one who can't
imagine.

I can reassure them that it only *seems* dark, on the *outside*.

Your eyes don't move, your head is as still as a hill in the distance.

I can't lie, but I can promise them it's no more than a *gentle tumble through a
night lit with windows*.

Just as a start. Until they're ready. Ready? you say. For more. Less

afraid. That, you say, is the trouble. That's what they can't imagine, only more
of the same, more of what they already know.

You have tried to explain this to me in so many different ways, and I've tried, I
really have, but I only seem to miss the point in a new way

every time. Then, I don't know how, but all of a sudden I've got traction, traction and momentum. I'll tell them it's like fireworks!

A short burst of stuttering bumps, then a splash. Like astronauts. A ticker tape parade and you're home free,

boasting one or two of your own little silken puckers, the immortal seal of an immortal's kiss.

You are amused at how literally impossible I am finding this.

They are not *scars*, I insist, unless you insist on seeing them as scars.

Yes, you say, but they're the ones, don't you see? But I don't see. I change my tack. I persist. There must be a way

to show them it's heroic. To ignore the locked doors and dark shutters banging their own paint off all night in the bone-cold,

salt-spitting wind. Though it gnaws at them like blank stares. Fixed. Pitiless. Pitying. Bottomless.

You are quiet now. You've stopped trying. But I can't stop.

There's an infinite sky behind the tawdry, scornful skyline and it's ablaze with the most beautiful, ephemeral, illuminating, eternal

illusions, night after night. I know, I know. It's a paradox. Surely they can understand a paradox.

And then I remember.

We've seen it, I remind you, you and I. Haven't we seen it?

You nod your head slowly, finally. Yes, you say. Yes, the Leonids.

Yes, the Leonids, I say. You remember. I look straight at you and close my eyes

and you are gone and they are here, the Leonids again

turning the parched December night into a vast, shimmering Atlantic

and we're back, you and I, in that first whole glorious sparkling summer
     morning

again and for a moment,

for an hour, sun-shed petals blanket the surface and the ocean

is the sky and the summer is

the morning and the fiery, rosy sunlight of every first summer morning is

on the water and the water is blinding

blinding in the light of its return

blistering as it burns in the return of that light

LEGO

When Shark Week rolled around again to remind us we had been out of our
    depth for months, we awoke

to find The Destroyer drinking tea in the kitchen we'd grown up with,
    inarticulate Hamlets popping in and out of the cupboards

as another fat Polonius scampered underfoot. That is, I was pretty sure we
    were only dreaming. *Hamlet*, you had recently

confided in me, is like LEGO. Every time you take it apart you can put it
    together another way. This time I was grieving

somebody else's grief, bumping into the furniture of words for feelings I had
    buried beneath tombstones

that turned out to be water lilies under an earth made of ice floes. Once, I
    could tell the difference, but now, now—

Was it even really love if what you really wanted was only for someone to be
    better? When they placed their hand

on your head, like a lily pad of benediction, the surface broke open like a
    walnut beneath a hammer blow

and I remembered having drowned too once, climbing the moonless sands of
    this world's broken hourglass.

The deeper I fell, the lower I climbed. How long I wore those dunes like a dun-
colored dress I would have to throw out

and grow into. Sometime it seems like the only way to learn is to unlearn.
Nobody does free-form LEGO anymore,

you told me, if they ever really did. Or puts on *Hamlet* without a script.
Sometimes, every week is Shark Week,

every morning The Destroyer, once again in the kitchen, is poking, again, at
the lid as if it were a can of Sanka.

As if it were only impersonating a lid. But you and I, who are on the inside,
we've seen the blade saw through it,

seen it circle in the sea like a fin in an upside-down sky or the stop-action tip of
an upside-down crown. The thing

to know, the thing to keep in mind, when you find yourself trying to find
yourself again, in among the weeds and words,

wading through shallows of ash among charred and splintered spars with a
mouthful of sand, is that it's only

when you reassemble them, from the inside, that you can finally grow to love
them, like the touchstone they always were

meant to be. Like the promise of lily pads. Whereas living in the opposite of
dreams only looks simpler,

but is only as solid as *Hamlet*, as safe as Shark Week, as real as those shadows
that keep moving

below the surface we all believe in

Inner Life

On a bad day, it cheers me no end to remember how you surprised everyone at
  the wedding breakfast postmortem

with your quiet reflection on the bride's new sister-in-law. She'd behaved badly.
  There'd been no question.

We'd all been dying to talk about it. But I can't imagine it occurring to anyone
  but you that she might have

no inner life. I can still see it rippling slyly around the table. She hasn't had an
  easy time of it, S— had countered,

as if it were an accusation. What even is an inner life? M— had asked. How can
  we know? B— had come back with,

and why does it matter? As for me, I remember thinking it was slightly unfair
  and entirely plausible. Please, don't try

to tell me how much she's suffered, you'd said as the eggs arrived. Maybe it was
  all the time you'd been spending

with Chekhov, whom you worshipped and called the master of narcissism. The
  epidemic he could not cure,

you'd said. Maybe that explains why he couldn't leave it. You yourself at that
  time obsessed with Goruv

and the difficulty of empathy. I can't decide, you'd said, if it's even possible to
    have empathy for someone

who stubs their soul on the same doorjamb every morning. Ouch, I think I'd
    said, but you shook your head. It's not the same

as the toddler the exasperated father finally buys velcro laces for, or teaches to
    rip the bandaid off, like a man.

Ouch, I said again and, after a pause, What about Anna? Meaning Goruv's
    beloved in the story. Anna? you smiled. Anna

is a mirror, like her name, where what is not identical is just reversed. For a
    Goruv, you'd said, facing me across the table, an Anna

is not another. She's nothing but an Echo. That pleased you. The way echo
    echoed nothing. An echo that goes on and on unheard.

So, I asked you, they don't love? Simpleton that I was. Then. Thinking we were
    having a conversation.

It is only their unhappiness that is indispensable, you'd replied. Your dimples
    twinkling briefly like raindrops under a streetlamp

only to disappear just as suddenly, swallowed by their own small splashes,
    unlike the baby teeth that fall in a clatter in the famous dream.

It's only a hunch, you'd said to us all that ominous morning. I hardly know her.
    I only saw what we all saw. And I know

I was not alone at the table worrying if my own inner life, or lack thereof, had
    been visible, like a slip, or imagining I held within me

the kind of riches and depth and complexity of an old wine, all going into shaping my outer life like a marvelous, or even a terrible, secret.

And then we all returned to the new day before us, trying to imagine a new conclusion for what was, after all, only just beginning

The Blank Day

The house at dusk is a different house. It is a different kind of house. The boy
we met, you and I, at the lake that summer,

who laughed too often, was a different boy from the one we had known the
summers before because we saw him

in a different kind of light, a new season hiding behind summer. His laugh
laughed with a new sweetness

and a new sadness. And though there was still genuine amusement in it, it was
no longer intact. There was a false—not false,

just new, a new abandon, more surrender than release, closer to something we
might call folly.

At Acquavella it was the roosters and the bulls that caught at our coat sleeves
and tugged at the hems of our attention,

making a new ruckus that came of an old terror, forcing the old pieces into
new places, a new order

out of an old disorder, which made it impossible to do the one thing they
deemed detrimental and seemed determined to be doing,

to be being rooster and bull. The tenderness in the portraits looked upon them
with renewed pity, called upon,

as they were, to perform rooster and bull, bull and rooster, for a new public,
   even in the privacy of domestic dissatisfactions

no place to call home. When Tina confided in us about just how difficult it had
   become to turn a profit during the pandemic,

she held my hand for a long moment, because we were sisters. Like my mother
   finding the words to represent my father

that did no violence to the living or the dead. The same kind of words she had
   found a hundred times before to hold the place

of the old order and leave a place for the new one, absent coercion.

Within the fields of color there is a time of day and a time of year and we find
   all the old paintings in the new ones,

ourselves standing before them in a new awe to be discovering more layers,
   more fields, more color. You have always

held art shows to us a different way of seeing, but I think now it's not us, we
   don't change in our ways, but the truth

of things, that's what changes, and we, we can't do anything about that beauty,
   which is not afraid of fear

like the house at dusk, when the colors of the day are everywhere and
   disappearing, even where I can't see them

Forsan et Haec Olim Meminisse Iuvabit

The ospreys have departed. I've been watching them all summer, running
down their victims, nursing their damp chicks like old wounds,

watching me. They've taken summer with them, leaving us summer's
shipwreck. It falls slowly into ruin, like the nest they've abandoned,
inherited by swallows.

There is nothing heartbreaking about any of this. I'm only curious to know
where they have gone to winter,

and how long they'll stay there.

They could, I read in the drowned pages of my new *Peterson's Guide*, already be
as far as Costa Rica,

astonished at how long it can take to recognize the things that can hurt us.

The gulls have no seasons. All year they climb and dive, dive and climb,
screaming and smashing

the shells they gather against the ledge. It's always the same small fury, as if the
clams were inept offers of help

that have done them no good at all, another idiotic set of beliefs that have
outworn their welcome and haven't the good sense

to pack their bags and go home. Tearing at what she feeds on one turns an
empty eye to me.

It's not me you have to worry about, I want to tell her.

The osprey is more civilized and more cunning. She flies past my kitchen
window clutching her prey in her briefcase,

a one-woman double-decker bus.

I imagine her landing her catch on her own kitchen counter, a fact no one can
question, a truth that no longer fights back.

How good we are to remember these things that once made us unhappy with a
different kind of sadness.

In the late afternoon sun, small pebbles cast shadows as long as love. I try to
remember without regret

who I was at the beginning of summer, as if I too sat atop a telephone pole
planted in the middle of a fine green marsh

surveying my defeats with a form of satisfaction, looking forward with the
kind of equanimity that rivals the platitudes of politicians

who, all summer, have been formulating their unassailable opinions to repeat
on repeat until they too are ripe for abandon

and the swallows are ready to make a home there for a short season,

or pull them apart for their own translations.

How Virgil must have loved that part of himself Aeneas stood for. Enough, I
think today, to burn the *Aeneid*.

That's what I fly home to you with in my own briefcase. I prop it open atop
your desk, knowing I have the advantage.

Since he's not here to prove me wrong, or prevaricate, I say, satisfied to gather
up the kindling like a nest to keep us warm all winter

Subtle Ties

It's like, you say, your hands clasped together tightly, taking a hammer to a
lightbulb in an effort to demystify a flower.

I blink involuntarily, as you've pointed out I always do at a violent image. Or
deflower a mystery? And make a joke.

The verbal blink, you call it, which I thought was good.

Your fingers peel away from the flesh they'd adhered to to cup the globed fruit
only you can see,

rolling open in an invisible magic trick to reveal—a bloom beneath the bulb!

We both marvel at the beauty of it, and your sleight of hands, before you let
them drop to your sides where they close

upon an unseen grip.

The trouble, you say, I sometimes think, stems from all the ways we use words
to do all the things we can't,

or that they can. Apart from music.

You mean truth, I know that. Because you are a poet and the Flannery
O'Connor story has gotten under your skin.

Steams? I try, extending a fraction of a smile, like a small hand to help you up a
sharp wall. Steams from?

Our eyes lock, but you don't bite. The walls of the soul. The barricades

of the soul. You turn away from me. The irony is beautiful, you say. You are
    bitter and facing the horizon

which has tricked me, seeming to lie along the top of the clouds.

She could have written it herself. Your hands fly to your eyes,

your ears, your lips, in a mock calisthenics. She who did not shrink from—
    Who looked every last word she ever wrote down

in the eye. I agree with you, but you aren't done. Who took the measure of
    every last one of her characters

and judged herself, as if they were her character, too—

You were conceding something to someone in your head. Pieces of her.

I'm not defending her, you say suddenly. That is, I am, but only because they've
    thrown her into the ring against the Cyclops.

You mean Polyphemus and the intruders in his cave, and the pot, and
    slamming down the lid.

It's like—you look down, rooting around in some dark burlap bag for your
    next metaphor, looking back up—

those families that are like cults.

There is a door flung open suddenly and you turn back to me. She never so
    much as flinched

at the dead bodies singing like a kettle in the basement, though if it hadn't
    been for her God—you shake your head.

And her mother, I try, again, though my heart isn't in it.

Love can be so ugly, you say. This is like when the celluloid used to sizzle and
burn up the actors' faces on the screen

and I know you are thinking about Hannah Arendt, but I am remembering
Ran, how no amount of goodness or wisdom

or wit could stop it, what one, small, dumb, relentless step sets like fire on its
path. No putting out the lies that want to be the truth,

no stronghold strong, no redoubt redoubtable enough.

A hammer has an eye, I remember then. And pianos have hammers.

A hammer has a cheek. That is your answer. Like the beast with red cheeks.

And a throat. And a claw. Yes, who would want to see that? I am remembering
Hidetora now, when he sees it all, maybe,

for a moment, and I had to turn away.

A flower has a stem, I offer, and steam flowers. I am singeing the tips of my
fingers on the last burning straws. I know it as well as you.

It only seems to, you, more gently now, almost gently. It used to power
engines, but not anymore.

The words evaporate, as all but the ones we think we can't agree on always do,

the way Kurosawa's clouds unravelled, emptied of mercy and meaning, as
silence and hooves hammered at the earth

and horsemen dove from their saddles in the rout, and horses flew riderless
across the screen and out of the light

III

I Do Believe Her

It was spring, she said, when a nightingale settled into a suitcase, open and
    empty as a new day, making her nest

in the middle of the freshman quad. Within hours of daybreak both
    nightingale and suitcase had been cordoned off

while experts were flown in and the ornithology department banned frisbees
    and speakers in windows. After a week or two

of gawping and journalists, the old routines resumed. Pedestrians once again
    flowed unimpeded in a stream

parting and meeting around the suitcase and her nightingale. You can believe
    me, she said, but I don't need you to believe me.

Then she told me that the suitcase didn't look like a suitcase, the way in
    dreams things don't look like themselves

but nevertheless are what they are. And although I never myself got a clear
    view of her, I knew she was there.

There are so many things we know without ever seeing them clearly.

It's also true that sometimes this makes them feel as though they never
    happened at all. Although, sometimes, the opposite.

I myself have owned and used many a suitcase for which there is no inventory,
   and which I no longer remember, but I remember

the one in college the nightingale found in the quad and made into her nest for
   a time like my own. Or a painting

I love that I can't reproduce or describe. Or an old tune I can't hum in a key or
   a shape you can hear, although I can

hear it. Sometimes I tell myself it was only a dream, a dream that has stayed
   with me in the form of a memory.

That seems fair, since memories often steal the form and feel of dreams.
   Equally they sing days open and closed like nightingales

and suitcases. And I, for one, have never trusted people who don't love
   suitcases any more

than the ones who always carry theirs with them, chained to their wrist, like a
   charm on a bracelet, or cut into bricks

with no zip compartments or garment bags that unfold like stories, but not as
   slowly as the truth.

To this day, I have more suitcases than I can count under the bed, and up in the
   loft, too. What I learned that spring

is that there are two types of myth. There's a myth like a suitcase and a myth
   like a nightingale, and you can always choose the one you can trust

One Small Sleep Past

We were talking about phaetons because I was rereading *The Portrait of a Lady*
   and you had seen one in Newport,

at the museum, a spider, or a high-flyer, you couldn't recall. It was before the
   pandemic and we were all

suffering from some form of amnesia. You might have been confusing it with
   the rig in Bath, purported to be

the very one that untimely transported poor old Thomas Warwick out of this
   life before he was able to write

the great poems of his maturity. Diana's poem about Nick Drake had very
   nearly brought me to tears on Zoom,

leading me to consider what it was I was really very nearly crying for. And you,
   you were telling me about the lavish, or exorbitant,

or rococo, you couldn't decide, wheels on which the open body of the carriage
   sat, lightly sprung,

which sounded like highly strung to me, which you allowed was also an apt
   description, they were so dangerous.

The wheels on the one you saw were yellow, like the sun. And it was there, out
    of that blue, that I remembered the fat bee

floating, like a choice or a far-off dirigible, in the early summer heat of the rose
    garden, at the Huntington, suspended

from the finest, least lavish, most silken thread of air. It had struck me, and
    stuck with me, like a stinger without the sting,

how he sat up on nothing but his haunches, his delicate forelegs pawing at an
    invisible door as if for some kind of mercy.

Or so I imagined, I imagine, perhaps because I had been listening to Lucinda
    Williams that morning singing about it on Erik's Spotify,

and we had overheard that couple speculating about billionaires disporting
    themselves like gods and dispensing mercy

or justice or wisdom, whatever they chose, and you had frowned, and I had
    bitten my lip, reminding me of another bee,

the bee that bit my lip for me on the grounds of the World's Fair, and that I was
    not yet qualified, being all of three, to bite it for myself.

How long some things last, unless they are called upon to mark the end, or the
    beginning, of something. Looking across

the table at you I found myself wondering whether I had stopped being that
    certain girl who always knew what she was really thinking.

All I could safely attest to was that lately, inexplicably, I had begun to stop
    trying to spin the world. Let it spin without you,

a voice seemed almost to be whispering in my ear. I think it was yours.

Maybe shame and mercy are related, as you always maintained, like the poles
of a magnet, repelling and reminding each other

of each other, since it can always go either way, like those who don't feel
themselves to have any power feeling empathy

for those with no power, or disdain, whether that's a feeling, or a choice, or a
justification.

Unless nothing tips the scales apart from the better part of balance. And
wasn't it a feat, all those years,

I wanted to tell you, balancing, if we did manage to balance, and I'm not sure
we did, sure as I was then, since now

I know that there are as many ways to trip without falling as flaws in the
sidewalk, and as many kinds of false.

But what I wanted to show you was me, all of thirteen, stepping into the pale
pink satin toe shoes that had hung, framed

like a portrait, or a gauntlet, and which I had waited so long to deserve what
could it matter how much I still wanted them?

Balanchine was Balanchine, she was saying, as I wound the double helix round
and round my small ankles, spinning and spinning

until I was the last one standing still, and the world, at last, both under and
around me, the only one doing the spinning for all of us.

It had been so long since I had given the benefit of the doubt to doubt, so busy
calling the web the story of my art, when really—

really—I was only hovering in between two worlds, one

in which I remembered your mother telling you to go on and pull your father's
    Mercedes out of the garage

and take it for a spin, you alone knowing how much she liked to play with fire,

and this other

Sanctuary

I know as soon as I wake up it's time to start rethinking everything again. First
of all it's New Year's day.

But that's not why. Nor the Wittgenstein that arrives in my inbox about the
limits of discoveries, serendipitous

as that is. It could be the dreams we've been dreaming, you and I, vivid and
ridiculous, like all the best dreams,

pieces of them sticking with us, or vice-versa, willy-nilly, like birthmarks, or
coming back out of their nowhere

like notes we posted to ourselves in the pockets of another life.

I still haven't told you, I tell you, about the day I visited the Underworld. Like
one of the classical heroes or poets, I clarify.

I didn't suppose you meant the criminal one, you joke, Pluto stepping
momentarily into the conversation as a kind of

crime-boss/godfather figure out of a *Law & Order* episode. There follows a
series of predictable jokes about counting and pomegranates.

But what I mean is the John Soane house, in particular its subterranean levels
rammed to the extremities with marble effigies

and death masks. They were bobbing like apples in a sea of alabaster, I tell you.
Porphyry, elegies, plaques,

urns, reliefs, granite. It was as if the line between one life and next, form and
matter, dream and not dream

had been completely eradicated, I say. By death? you counter. I saw Endymion,
I tell you by way of an answer,

the boy whose sleep did not just mock but met the death it played at.

Is that a quote? you ask without looking up. That's how I know I have your
attention. It's a vertical labyrinth, I say.

It wends downward.

Mr Soane, I think, thought of himself as a kind of posthumous Virgil, leading
his guests to his peace—I hold up the sign of victory—de la resistance.

I pause to allow you to appreciate my paronomasia. It's a sarcophagus, I
explain, set in its own sepulchral chamber. Remember

the yellow sapphire we couldn't take our eyes off of? I remember, you say. Well
this was nothing like that.

You expel air through your nose like a stallion. It did, I say, remind me in a way
of Pakal's tomb. Pakal, the great general

in the Archaeological Museum in Mexico City, whose death mask seemed to
have been pieced together

out of the jade shivers of what had once been something whole, beautiful and
intact. And I knew you were remembering too

how it couldn't take its empty eyes off us. How we stood there, still but for the
   motion of our breathing,

reflecting the black abyss he stared straight into.

Wasn't that the day you visited Rita? you interrupt, scrolling through the abyss
   of your phone.

High up on the fourteenth floor, I answer in my head and, out loud, While she
   was peeling her daily grapefruit,

telling me how grateful she was it was south facing. The room, not the
   grapefruit, I assume, you interject, without looking up,

and I don't break my stride either, Saying, I can eat them while I'm here since
   I'm off the statins. Like Proserpine, I say then.

The more you sleep the more you sleep, you once told me, and I guess that
   goes for seeing as well, and my feeling

that there is an order to everything, even if it's different for everyone. But like
   cells, I suppose, the order can go awry.

And it isn't until much later, days later, after rethinking it all again, from the
   beginning, that I begin to see

that there is a kind of death that separates words from their meanings, and
   people

who live on a surface without knowing, that is, feeling, the ground, even if it's
   made of the indefatigable depths that wend

and slosh and sway fourteen floors below. And that that is different from
   dreaming, or forgetting.

And that's when I see, not with my eyes but, as Diane says we can, with my
   skin, that I have forgotten again,

with all that you do for me so present to me, that you are still, of course, as if
   time has anything to do with it,

thinking about all the people you think I want you to be

Alive Again

I must have gotten out on the wrong end of Park, since if it wasn't from having
to make my way all around the western perimeter

of Grand Central Station, why was I flustered? There were still times I just
couldn't tell whether I was facing north

or south, still only learning to infer the source of light from the depths of the
shadows. In other words, if I weren't already looking back

from the evening ahead, how would I be able to find the words? Something
already indelible was already smoothing itself back

into the unruffled surface even as it was making its appearance, like mullet,
the thinking woman's fish,

if that's the one that jumps. Or the empty glass once the froth has popped and
the beer is finished.

Don't make too much of any of it, I was telling myself. The words can go either
way. False leads like crumbs of wishes.

What the name of the bar you'd chosen would mean I wouldn't know until the
end of the story.

Of all the conversations at the bar only the two of us were having, only the
current was more able to hook its own drift,

and yet you said you could remember everything you'd ever said to me,
  forgetting everything you wanted to ask me.

Forgetting is the wrong word. This was too far back. And I heard myself saying
  that it was only because I didn't understand

how it worked, that's what made it interesting. This I knew I meant, my
  doubts confirmed it, and maybe they didn't know either.

Wake up and smell the beer, that's what you were telling yourself, alive again,
  the flying through those waters like coming to

after drowning, sputtering to comprehend what was this light, salt water
  bruising your eyes, your, your—But maybe

it was just one of those things you never hear until you repeat it back again,
  and commit to something more than memory,

like the name of this bar, or come to your senses

Why We Love

I've been thinking about the cynics again, you confessed with a hangdog look.
 We were on our way home,

having spent a long night among the phonies. At least they're not hiding who
 they're not. I knew you were thinking about bitterness,

how it lies like sweetness. A shriek of self-preservation arrived from the edge
 of the water and I wanted to tell you

as I saw you smile, there and then, just how much I have always loved your
 own cynicism, filled as it is to overflowing with yearning

and knowing, and to remind you how long ago we had gripped each others'
 hands so tight as we marveled together at the scene

in the funhouse in *The Lady from Shanghai*, and I heard you whisper, What if
 that's love?

but we had been driving for hours by then. And in the late-morning light along
 the rocky coast not far

from home, I turned to where the geese and the egrets feed. And it was the
 grace of the egret I was contemplating

when you said, From themselves, I mean. With "the cynics," at least you know
 where you stand, because they know

where they do. The gulls began to scream at the geese then, gerrymandering
   their clam beds, and I wanted

to know whether "the phonies" are ever earnest about anything, but we had
   reached the last familiar bends,

and you were smiling so sadly, as if forgiveness were off the table

The End of Summer

I know that he's great, a genius, but he's just too lush, too ardent, too full-on. I
    just can't play, or even listen

to him any more. We had been talking about Mozart, but this was Brahms,
    and the quiet violinist sitting to my left.

There had been a trio playing during the service but he had not been a party to
    that, and there was an altogether

different kind of music behind the happy chatter and plink of silver and china
    now. On my right, a woman commenting

on the end of summer, so long in coming. Beethoven you can't avoid, he
    admitted, smiling gently, all his wrinkles twinkling,

but the late quartets, they—his eyes dove like a hawk and returned all
    kindness—are so angry.

He offered the words like bread and smiled again, a smile shielding a wince. I
    don't do well with anger, he admitted.

I considered his locution, and who did do well with it. Ice in the birdbath,

the woman was saying, over my shoulder, which I had had a weird
   premonition I would find, probably

on account of the unwonted quiet. But I was trying to focus on Mozart, and
   anger, even somebody else's,

and how it can suddenly play back to life like an air, and who Beethoven was in
   the mild violinist's,

and who was Brahms. Mozart is so clear, so full of clarity and light—he smiled
   a new smile, there was mischief in it—

the perfect marriage of logic and feeling. He had a whole wedding party of
   smiles, and I had never thought

this way about taste before. Themes, yes, of course. We all search out our
   themes. Or keep tripping over them,

but the hands of ghosts we want to hold on to, or hide from, this was a new
   twist, or wrinkle, in a longstanding conversation.

I always take it wrong. The woman behind me again. Like an oboe taking up
   her burden and drawing me away from the melody,

the banks of the river whose rocks and roots I was trying to cling to, still
   smiling my one smile at the sweet-tempered soul

who couldn't listen to Brahms, as if it were somehow a provocation. Like the
   bad fairy and her gift at the christening,

though I never know what they mean, or think they mean, when they say it.
   And across the table, a debate

over whether the old classic Ken Burns documentary about the Civil War was
more beautiful than this new one.

Countries are like the sorceress Medea, they kill their own children to get
something back, or to get back to something

they've lost hold of. Or at somebody. Using gold, gold and jealousy, jealousy in
the older sense, the way the tertium quids

are said to have professed *Jealousy, Argus-eyed jealousy of the patronage of the
President*. But everyone always

thinks everyone else knows what they mean and that they don't understand
them.

When I listen to Brahms I feel alive. I hear anger sometimes when I listen to
Beethoven, but I don't feel anger,

or afraid. And as for Mozart, wasn't it wit, the way a change on a face or the
color of words can amuse and astound you,

a sudden season usurping the nest the way only an heir can? The violinist
reminded me so much of your father

I found myself wondering if he liked Beethoven, because, although he didn't
do so well with anger either

he had made a sort of peace, if you can call it that, with his own, and was that a
curse, like the angry fairy's,

or some imperfect marriage of logic and feeling? Or was it more like winter
coming on late finally,

like the morning you wake up to a more silent silence and ice in the birdbath,
   and whether he had ever said, one way

or the other, and even if he had, whether like so many statements people
   make, smiling the smile they may

think is their one true smile, there was more than a premonition in it

Mỹ Sơn Sanctuary

First the thunder shrugged, like the old man who would not lower his price in
    Hoi An. It was like the beginning

of the nursery rhyme we used to embroider into nonsense and air. But that
    came later, some time after

we cleared the cloud-soaked stronghold where the children stood, soles
    planted, blowing like antennae on the rooftops

of the abandoned arsenal. All our reading and research was only going to get
    us so far. Whatever we had imagined,

having heard tell of the storied temples scattered like families in the sunless
    jungle, vanished in the red, dusty paths

fanning out like trade routes. In the guidebook's map north was where we
    were now. The lines threading from Here to Java,

Kandahar, Cairo, reminded me of your hands, and the arc of flight paths out
    of Newark, and you of the pliant ribs of the lanterns

we made in the workshop in Hoi An. Is it so hard to keep the order clear
    because so much happens at once? I couldn't elude

the nervous woman, her eyes darting like swallows at sundown sitting among
the saffron fishing nets as the thunder cleared

its throat. She looked like someone we knew but couldn't put our finger on,
caught between seeing and remembering,

saying nothing again and again. That was after we clambered over those rocks
the size of ostrich eggs in Hue, breaking spider webs,

the lone bird repeating her piteous lament all but inaudible over the agitated
crests of the cicadas thundering down like cataracts

in Shostakovich. To my ear at least, there was more of self-pity in it. You asked
if it was because they remind us of the illusion

of our most cherished certainties that we are drawn to ruins and Ahn said, The
way some are drawn to war. When we were young

of course we didn't realize just how much has to do with trade routes, I
thought, when Ahn explained what it meant

to find the Yoni Linga so far north. The thunder growled just next door then
and Ahn pointed out the dark bricks no one knows

how to make anymore. Like Iznik blue, we said as one. New bricks, he
clarified, were made of a rose-colored dust mixed with a resin

that becomes toxic in the rain. That explained why the small group of
bricklayers were packing up, patches of the wall

blazing golden, as if sunbeams were falling on the old temples from a fiery,
nonexistent sun, or one reaching down through the ages of the treetops,

from something like the past. That was when, finally, the thunder seemed to
     dredge something up, the way you sometimes think you can

hear someone thinking, like a click in the jungle in between the tattered
     battalions of the words they line up and

Fire! I tried to imagine what it was, and the shooters hiding among the hush
     and tangle of vines and ruins as the rain

began to splatter the pale dry ground and the dark thick leaves all around us,
     and what it might mean for me to have a memory of war.

We stood silently on the ledge of the craters in the earth the shape of death
     where the blasts had shaken the foundations

of what they failed to destroy. But most of all, I remember the rain, when it
     finally flowered in an outburst of fury in fists and drums.

By then we had taken refuge below the waves of the corrugated roof of the
     noodle house Ahn had brought us to. It means brother

he told us, sheepishly, Ahn. If I were a liar I would say it fell like gunfire, but
     what I heard were seeds, seeds

scattered in a deafening springtime as they pattered and ricocheted against
     those steely furrows in that furious finale

and I watched Ahn, smiling patiently as he demonstrated how to push the
     greens under and under the raveled strands

of the delicate nest floating in that small fragrant sea, blooming from a secret
     spring at the bottom of the earthenware bowl in our hands

IV

4'33"

1

It was spring again and the ants were back. A perforation on the march. The
brittle strand advancing

yet another false conclusion to winter. Tear here, they were saying, with their
uncomfortable silence. I was tempted

to hum them a few bars of John Cage, read to them from an Emily Dickinson
in a Morse Code they could relate to,

rearrange their stick-figure bodies with a flick flick flick until they were vertical
and emblematic, ready to form

a wretched, tattered, Tartar Grande Armée in retreat back to the garden door
from the kitchen I would learn

to call Moscow. But they were intransigent. How had I ever dreamed it could
be otherwise? Hadn't I already

seen in them a shadow of the string of pearls that had burst like a star-crossed
star inherited from the grandmother we knew as Alice

hidden behind the skirts of a saint named Theresa. And abracadabra, presto
change-o, here she was again,

in a poem, after all this time. And here was me still feeling bad for having felt
    nothing standing outside the door

of her house in Vienna. Not nothing. A desire to feel something. But what?
    Death is different

2

It was the spring we were back in Studio City, another transparent, Rothko-
    blue, L.A. morning,

the sidewalks flickering frame by frame like a film made out of films filled with
    actors and characters

each of us has countless times stepped into and out of. It's never a very
    welcome diagnosis. An apricot

Mustang parked at the curb. The same thing that did for Hvorostovsky

3

The soldier, in full dress, who played taps, reminded us of him, when he played
    the Count di Luna

in his final performances of *Il Trovatore*. Do you remember his pianissimo? It
    was just like the movies,

the way they danced their accordion quadrille until the king-size flag had
    shrunk to a pocket square

or a puck, like the ones we'd made out of nothing more than a sheet of spiral
    notebook paper

and flick flick flicked the length of the dining room table, a nose or an ear
   coming to precarious rest

to peer down just over the far edge into the abyss. It was the other one who
   marched toward us, offering the crownless cushion

to my mother, his white-gloves like a clamp holding a chair leg until the glue
   dries, a simile made for my father,

who had his own mind, of course, another of those things so obvious they can
   be hard to remember

4

Waking up in California, that rush of hopefulness when, for a fluttering
   moment, infinitely expanding, fleeting,

you forget everything, is the opposite of shouting in the theatre, which, you
   tell me, is how actors and directors

tell everyone they have no idea what it is they're supposed to be feeling. Just
   like in real life, we'd joked.

And isn't that funny! Since all this while I've been wanting to tell you about the
   storyteller, who came from Nova Scotia,

having lived in Newfoundland, and whom we met at the Neue Galerie, on line
   for schnitzel, in the middle

33

of the Ring Cycle. They had come, she and the math professor, for their
   thirtieth anniversary, but it was with more

than professional courtesy when he let her tell all the stories. And this is the
thing. What I wanted to tell you. Because

she spoke so quietly, it was as if after spending, no, filling, after filling so many
years with so many stories, she knew

exactly, as if everything she told us was *exactly*, how she was feeling. Now I
regret that we didn't ask her to tell us

one, or just the start, but at the time all we wanted to know was how could she
possibly remember

so many. Oh, she told us, it's the opposite of remembering. Every story is like a
new city or an old forest. You have

to get lost inside it. Lose all the words you once pretended to understand.
Then you can begin

to find your way out. Otherwise, she said, leaning in and growing confidential,
they only get the better of you.

Since she could see by our rapt faces that we weren't following, she added, at
her precise volume

just this side of inaudible, The key is to try to forget that you are trying to
remember. Each of us imagined then

a new worm discovering she can spin silk, the smooth oyster at her first taste
of grit, a green branch

forming her first difficult bud, a speck of the cold and clouds and dust out of
which whole star systems are born.

Otherwise, she said, sitting back in her chair and scattering every other sound
in the cafe with a wave of her hand,

it's all for nothing. And, I swear to you, we both saw it, the handful of rotting
seaweed torn from the sea

left to fade in the colorless sunlight just out of reach of the pearls of foam
hanging and melting beneath it

on the immutable strand, both heard the distant thunder of Napoleon's army
in retreat, the frozen snap snap snap

under boots, and the piano finally releasing the last note into the silence
waiting like a child at the door listening

for it to fall into the no sound, then the echo of no sound, nothing taking its
place except the marching, the endless marching

and singing that keeps vanishing down the cold road into the long Russian
winter

Nonesuch
Island

It had something to do no doubt with how long it had been since I had taken
  the leap off the side of a boat

into an ocean. Not that I had done any leaping that particular morning, small
  steps, aft in fact, leading

steppingly into bottle-green waters swinging gently like a thousand
  pendulums. And something, too, the next day after

with the hypnotic roar of the wind, the febrile thunder of the incessant
  Atlantic. God,

the racket. Like a storm without the storm, the elements snorting and
  stamping in a display of pure passion

leading nowhere. But I wasn't fooled. I could hear my own mind in it, turning
  over and over, like an engine

destined to idle in limbo forever, or the preposterous sputtering of the Italian
  coffeemaker Price had made the coffee with

before we took the boat out. But really, it was like none of those. That was just
  how we got to talking about trespassing

and cahows on the golf course, and the briny swell of the lush, green links, and
whether that had always been

Mr Macdonald's intention. And it was that very night, at Tucker's Point, as if
in illustration, that you, fed up with my

perfectionism, and in cahoots with the waitstaff, as if I didn't know, as a way
around my obstinacy, went around me.

And I, I was stumped. Why wasn't I angry? Until the next day at the edge of all
that self-defeating, purposeless

bluster of Aeschylean wind and Old Testament waters—Because the
November sun was so strong and it was such a perfectly

lovely day, and there was nothing that could ever mar or misshape it. And
when, after we returned home,

you bought the house slippers, to make it up to me—Not that either one of us
would ever say so. It was Price,

wasn't it, after telling us about the cahows, who said it was precisely those
things that were most worth stepping out of.

There wasn't anything remotely like it

Nest

The body is a nest, that's what Gil, my yoga teacher, says, though what he
means is something of a mystery.

The body is a home, perhaps, for birds can stand

for who we are those moments, rare but fine, when we take flight and,
unexpectedly (it's always unexpectedly)

break into song. Even when, it happens to us all some time, we lay an egg,
proving we remain

tone deaf and, alas, earthbound, in spite of everything. Or maybe only after all,
because I'm sure

that when we dream we all have perfect pitch and sound like Sutherland or
Pavarotti.

Even an ostrich who ought to know better dreams that she can fly.

For vipers too, I guess. We all have come across more than our share. That is,
our share. That is, we've harbored them within.

Does Gil mean them? When I think of a nest it's somehow high-cloud soft and
comfortable, more mist than cloud,

like the morning stuff I've seen roll down the mossy sides of hills, although I
know the moss is really treetops

hiding boughs and twigs, which are the bones of trees under the mossy flesh of
  leaves.

So we are trees as well as nests! I'm sure Gil knows.

When I *say* nest I think a thing that spins like clay beginning to take shape and
  grow

taller and more slender on a potter's wheel, or water going down a drain while
  coming out the faucet steadily, tornadoes

wobbling like children's tops to skitter back and forth across the Great Plains
  on TV, and cowboys,

lassoes whirling overhead, the dervishes and dancers of the West, which
  always takes me back to Destiny.

I'll have to say to Gil that he's a poet who knows the body is a home for dreams
  that are like ostriches and doves

and traitors twisting in the grass that is the breast; for all that holds on to a
  grudge as for dear life; for all we lose and loose

upon ourselves; all that disappears; the fledglings of the sinews and the blood,
  if blood is hope, and sinews

what holds hope in sight, like something we could lasso with a rope; and all
  that slips our grip and does not die,

both good and bad. For who we are, although we are not birds, when we are
  birds that sing for emperors

and dancers in the storm. For who we would but may never become. For what
  we visit in the name of love

upon our own. The lengths of string, stray feathers, strips of tinsel, buttons, treasured spurs,

all that we store, catch up and stumble on, from which we fly and which encumber us, to which we can't return.

I'll have to tell him that there's even more I've missed, more I'm missing still, although I also understand

when he says the body is a nest, he means a mystery, and that is something else

Not in Those Exact Words

You remind me of me, that's what he is saying, and I see us reflected in a dark
   window the coming winter of night

has turned into a mirror, whirling and spinning like dance partners at a fin-de-
   siècle Viennese ball. Not in

those exact words of course, but that's the gist nonetheless, the honest ghost
   in the irreversible machine.

We are standing in an eddy of cocktail party chatter. Self-possessed smiles and
   hired crystal tinkle politely

in lieu of a soundtrack. Not for the first time, I am happy enough to chalk it up
   to the influence of the spirits. If

the well-mannered din is any indication, the entire room is in high spirits.
   Dialogue and laughter ribbon

and linger like the shredded fog that hangs among the trunks and intermittent
   limbs where (was it just this afternoon?)

Munch's solid, ghostly figures stared out at us inconsolable from their lurid,
   frozen hells-on-earth. They have found themselves,

you said, at one of those junctures, as I turned to you, where they see some
canvas beyond the canvas of what has come

of their lives. Together we contemplated the leafless wood stopped dead in its
tracks on its descent to the door of the water.

Children are not just for Christmas tolls past like a bell of crinoline. It is a
grave error to understand your lover too well—

Like cardamom and fish tails. Imperceptibly I am overtaken by a sleep-like
stupor, leaden arms powerless to brush the silvery cobwebs

from lashes and legs of bronze like clock hands in the enchanted castle of a
family under a curse, my entire frame fixed now

on a scene in black and white shimmering with heat somewhere beyond the
scene. A fractured circle

and headlamps inundating the center like trumpets listening into a more
compact circle of grass and dirt and weeds

and hold your breath to hear the next swing of the small, soft, disembodied
bell,

the sound that rises like smoke from a Victorian chimney buried in the song of
the ground.

You have to open your own eyes to see from somebody else's. Aren't you always
telling me that?

How the greatest actors *embody*, and the lesser *disappear*. The frantic hand that
sweeps away the fog on the mirror

only to uncover a fresh shadow. How you laugh on the way home at what I had
heard as if I had seen it,

the unmistakable disappointment on their faces. The slow sad dawn, you call
   it, but a dawn none the less.

No, alas, children are not dolls, or train sets, not in those words, of course,
   although, as you add,

rather judiciously I think, even once the ship settles onto her eggs like some
   great bird onto the nest of the seabed,

there are still so many who never swim to the porthole. And as I fall asleep in
   the nest of our bed,

the room wheeling and swishing like a hoop skirt through flutes of
   champagne, the idea

that what he meant was that I put him in mind of a part of himself he had left
   behind forms like a picture.

That's the polite way of saying it, I think, dreamily, as if we were still talking.
   The ghost of himself is another.

You and I, that is, speaking without speaking, the way we are waltzing while
   we lie there, which means we aren't,

and what does that mean? And I can see him then, coming forward out of
   some old darkness,

to pull his own child up out of some true, untrammeled scrub, the generous
   spotlight contracted to a pinhole of empty stage,

the dark wells of his eyes no longer able to hear what he himself is saying,

the ghost of a smile breaking among the tinkling glass

The Porpentine and Quill

I will never forget that drive we took up Ben Lawers on our way through the
Grampions.

It was late autumn, late afternoon when we gathered everyone to show them
the incomparable view

from a small turnout on the northwest access, our secret vista, the one we had
discovered during one of our earliest visits,

and had only recently rediscovered and which we were sure everyone was
missing. Not that it was at all likely,

at that time of year, that they would see it, and indeed we drove straight into as
milky a sea of brume as any any of us

had ever encountered, so that for the rest of that treacherous drive we didn't
see much of anything else.

But like so many such wrongheaded excursions, this one did lead to the
wonderful story the Norwegian woman told us all

over nightcaps that wintry evening once we finally arrived and settled into the
cosy Free house where we always stayed.

What was her name? Solveig? Synnøve? Everything else we remember. It was
about the night the power went out

in the Emergency Room in the small industrial village she hailed from during
a flu epidemic. The generator had failed

and the entire staff was home in bed, having been struck down by the selfsame
flu, apart from one lone doctor,

a remarkable person, who, it later emerged, had never passed the exams, and
yet somehow, nevertheless, in the dark,

and wholly unassisted by man, woman or machine, since even back-up staff
could not be roused and summoned

from the neighboring village—there was no one left standing who could do
it!—had single-handedly juggled:

a three-car accident, a case of anaphylactic shock, a stroke, an overdose, the
delivery of a set of premature identical triplets...

All, moreover, while coming down with the same ravaging flu. A modern-day
miracle, she had said. Vigdis? Vilduk?

Everything else, clear as a bell. And furthermore, it eventually transpired that
this vessel, this superhuman exemplum,

was also a junky, an out-of-control control freak, who, more than anything
else loved the freewheeling free-fall, as she described it.

Silje? Unni? With its overwhelming feeling, as it's been described in more than
one reputable and oft-cited journal,

of no longer having to feel out of control. Which couldn't be so easy, I
    remember her saying. Turid? Ekmel? Bodil?

In this crazy, out-of-control world. I mean, I remember she asked us, the fire
    crackling and hissing, throwing fistfuls of shadows

that danced with and around us, how is it even possible? How can anyone
    control what is out of their control? And, as I recall

clearly, tracing with my finger through the window's inner fog the names the
    night had traced in the outer fog with hers,

we couldn't think of one thing that wasn't

The Raw and
the Cooked

At dinner the talk is all baseball. I try not to nod off. The semi-serious man
    with a season box

at Yankee Stadium is telling one of his stories. It's a tense night behind home
    plate and he's right there,

with two old friends, two writers—Who? I ask; I am the only one who seems
    to want to know. Paul

Auster, he says, with a question mark. And, I say, the whole word a question.
    And Don DeLillo. Can I be

the only diner who bats an eye? Trust the process you used to say, in oracular
    mode, which sounded

good, and yet there remained that sticky wicket, like death, that always
    stumped me, to wit: how do I know

this is part of the process? To which you would pitch that oracular nod that
    said, You have much to unlearn,

saying something equally inscrutable. So when I heard it again last night, the
    eternal question, on Second

Avenue, from the next table, in one of its more fugitive forms, I sought you
out, in my mind, not understanding

why, but knowing it was before you I should lay this question, like an old-
fashioned bat. About this, at least, I was not wrong.

Because, you said, he's bitter. And because they are his heart.

It reminded me of the first time, in my early twenties, and if I'm honest for a
good long while after, when, whenever I woke up,

I began to dream of cooking food raw. It was the burnt toast, I now suspected,
looking back like a pitcher

contemplating the runner over my left shoulder, the smell of it, and how long
it had taken me to think,

Is someone smoking? Or else: A stroke? Which, eventually, led me, after a
sudden swing of deliberation,

to determine that it was when you lost your sense of smell, that was the first
sign. I wouldn't miss it again.

Put on the light, you liked to say, like Othello's better angel, that's the key.
Some doors open, some doors won't.

They may open later. And as for possession, it's not like memory, not at all.
Even lost, it has permanence. Only now

I wonder if you were talking about the baseball cards in the secondhand shop
we had to go all the way

back up the Taconic for, which you no longer recalled, or the violet lampshade
I still regret leaving behind

how many moves ago? The very same shade of violet as Mrs Marotta's eyes. In
my mind. Where she still stands

in the glare of the afternoon sun by the door of the classroom, shading them
with her hand, like a visor, watching the straggler.

Even as a credulous seventh-grade child, I have always been a woman like Mrs
Marotta, without regrets.

The clearer they are, the stronger they burn, the harder it is to tell them apart.

I never did completely work out what you meant by that one. True memories
from false? Your memories from mine?

Even the made-up ones are true, you chime in. Even now. In my mind. Your
sibylline smile set in the smooth stone

of your finely chiseled lips. But I was already thinking about the wildflowers
we picked how many lives ago?

Petals sun-bright and beckoning in the pale hay mist by the side of the road,
and now I lay the piercing whorls

of apricot among the unripe bursts of raspberry, setting the cornflower
panicles powdery and delicate as moth wings

cheek by jowl with the egg-yolk eddies among the velvet dusky violet rings, like
that other kind of iris,

and cradled them in my lap the whole ride home, dreaming, or so perhaps I
imagined even then,

what it would feel like to come upon a whole meadow of them, those sole,
wild, pristine thoughts

you could be sure were all your own, and trying to remember the vase I put

them in

Conversations
We Never Had

It was while we were doing the dishes, Stewart washing and I drying, making
   neat stacks of clean dried plates.

Everyone is sensitive. That was Stewart. And I said, No, balking at the idea,
   not the idea—Yes,

everyone. Murderers, cynics, terrorists, tyrants, passive fathers, selfish
   mothers. He was right, I knew, but it was the word,

sensitive, which means something, suggests something, like consciousness,
   and, I would say, spills over into something

like empathy, and what Stewart meant, flipping each dish under the running
   water like a switch before handing it to me,

I also knew, of course, was having feelings. With an overtone of the way
   certain animals, and even plants

are sensitive. As in, to light. Though, and this is what stopped me, in even that
   sense, still, I imagined, feeding a plate

like a wheel making a sudden turn through the towel, the word itself balked,
   rebelling against being corralled

into that other pen with those others who didn't deserve it. Not because they
   didn't have feelings, we all have feelings,

but because they couldn't imagine the feelings of others, or even that anyone
   else had feelings, and therefore couldn't take

the feelings of others into account. But, the dishes done, we had already taken
   up other topics. And it wasn't until this morning,

while I was taking my run around the reservoir, which, from the air, someone
   said recently, I don't think it was Stewart,

or even that evening, looks like a bruise, that I remembered that I hadn't
   actually said any of that out loud

and realized, which isn't the same thing at all, with a start, which is another
   funny way of saying something (because

until you've been startled, you don't really begin?) that was another
   conversation we never finished

Monument Mountain

Cushioned and mildly inclining, like an accommodating auntie, the path back
down rolled like a ball and the world became smooth

and shady again as we landed mute strides into dumb earth, our breathing
neither labored nor rising and falling in that deep

contentment of sleep, when I turned in the suddenly dark wood as if called by
name to find myself gazing into the battered heart

of the deeply gouged, tobacco-leaf bark of an ash. The resemblance was
startling, audible. *This tree looks like Auden!*

As if someone had said it aloud. As if I had been walking these woods all these
years endeavoring to work out what it was,

exactly, Auden reminded me of, and finally, like the improbable lightning of
the lottery, Eureka!, it had struck. Of course! Auden

looked like, and therefore was like, the trunk of a tree.

I was still trying to decide what kind of photographer I was, although I am not
a photographer. But my initial answer

to Bob's question a few days earlier had perplexed me. Are you macro,
portrait, wide-angle, 150mm, landscape, telephoto…?

I was still wondering if it was a trick question, like the sound of the tree in the
forest no one can hear, still in awe of all the many ways,

like Homer's muse, our houseguest had found to tell us what he was like. But
hadn't I flinched from telephoto like a snide remark

smacking of flashy yachts and topless celebrities on the Riviera? And yet here I
was zooming in on tree bark as if it were the face of a poet

I had, unbeknownst to me, been looking at as the answer to a question I
hadn't known I had been asking.

Did everything always come back to this dogged affection for presumption, in
spite of how many more truly

intriguing ways there were to approach everything? And of being like, in spite
of it always meaning being unlike

at the same time? Did it matter that they were both, what we're like and what
we like, only fancies?

For we had been descending, triumphant, from the momentary peak, sharp
and unyielding, exposed to the penetrating appraisal

of the sun, and to which we, groping on hands and feet, had arrived, having
done the hard, paradoxically satisfying work of not knowing

what we were after, and yet somehow, that solid-seeming triumph paled beside
this pale, convoluted idea

of Auden's face, that it was marked by his life, until he came to resemble an as-
   if speaking tree

in the soft woods on the return from the summit, the summit of an
   unpresuming, prepossessing marker of a mountain

in Melville country, Melville and Hawthorne, as if they were both themselves

trees slipping back into the landscape they had momentarily stepped away
   from to take the measure of.

And rather than relinquish the whole notion as a prop, a toy,

I preferred to have been saved by an English poet,

one who had seen more than even he could find all the words for, or some
   other likeness

The International Banana Museum

A CODA

Sometimes all you have to do is find the rent, and pay it apart

How can you tell the difference between what you want to say and what you want to happen? Between what you want to happen and what you want to know?

You aren't merely riddling. Memory, it is your most recent theme, or peeve, is either pure fiction, from which we can learn, or creative non-fiction, *sic*.

We pause at the glass case, the Glaskasten as you call it, flashing your Nietzsche. It contains the murky photograph of a tall man in a dark suit standing beside

a small woman in a floral dress on top of what looks to be the Old Aswan Dam. We are briefly baffled by the empty label.

The trouble, you were saying, is that we call our feelings memories, as if we were not the authors of both, or were the authors of either.

The woman in the dungarees who has come in just ahead of us chooses that moment to declare that she has never liked Fontana.

Take the rift, you continue, registering your approval, between reasons and
    intentions. We all have our reasons, we always have our reasons; whereas,

the machinery of intentions is an altogether different story, since even the
    unintentional is often a type of intention.

We stop to contemplate the matchbox Firebird parked between a sleeping pile
    of Monopoly money and one of the Empress Shōtoku's

million white pagodas, and another blank label. Explanations are always
    suspect, explanations are always upsetting.

You pull a colorized postcard of Piero's *Resurrection* out of a box. Indignation
    is always suspect, indignation is always suspicious.

I lift a black-and-white postcard of Magritte's *Apple-Picking in Springtime* out of
    another.

The rigid compass of what we hear we fashion out of what we want to hear.
    Out of the magnificent scenery of expectations we embellish

the unencumbered moment. That's when we find the cowboy boots and the
    scrappy strappy sandals the color of the midnight desert sky

in unmarked boxes and exactly our sizes. Consider, you offer, the deliberate
    disguise as against the sufficient cause, the play

as against the delusion. Without discussion we take sides behind the opposing
    forces of toy soldiers set out on the billiard table with planters

in the pockets and burgundy baize. Through the frond leaves you whisper
    about the wedge that is driven, invisible as Adam Smith's left hand,

for which no one need take credit, and we laugh out loud at the absence of any
    label whatsoever. For there are so many ways strife can be useful,

you opine, suddenly solemn, running a finger along a crack in the suddenly
    low ceiling, even on a small scale.

And as for the hairline fracture between how we interpret what is said and
    what we don't want to believe, you say, looking toward the next room,

we can turn it to the wall like a quarrel. Like the quarrel between the sum total
    of the life we believe we are about to begin living

and the rogue, incremental, half-undecided, gently crumbling gardener's
    cottage. The failsafe conundrum as to whether it is the symbol that walks

the dog or the dog that walks the symbol. Fracture zones, you seem
    unexpectedly to remember, bear the names of their research assistants,

so called. Just think of the void between Piero's Christ and the soldiers, you say
    then, pointing to the arrow pointing through a small doorway,

which may be the difference between life and death, more difficult to split than
    the Adam from the Eve. And as I climb the diminishing circular staircase

behind you, you call down: Under every rock lies an old coin, behind every old
    coin, the new moon, with its two dark sides.

As for the gulf between the dream the soldiers are dreaming and the dream
    they are living, you say, shrugging as I reach the small landing

at the top of the house, to fathom it there would have to be friction. Through
    the darkness, a two-story dollhouse rises up like a cloud

upon a pedestal, with windows on weekends like snapshots of happiness, but
without labels or doors. You have returned to Piero and what you call the
incongruity

between what he's seen (his right eye) and what he's seeing (his left). Therein,
you sigh, heavily, lies the longest road to Damascus, that is, to pity

from fear. How can we even begin to measure the abyss between the infinite
sadness behind his expression and the infinite horror within it?

Wherein how he came to be thus and the thus he came to be. Which is no
different, in its way, from the breach between what we know

and what we would happily assert as knowledge.

The indivisible divide between the addends and the sum.

The chasm between what is representative and whom and what that
representative represents.

Between what we can't know and what we can't assume, the incalculable drift

and all the appreciable disparities among the various sources of light, the
inconceivable discrepancy between two distinct vanishing points.

On the Formica counter, we find fruit in the fruit bowl.

There are always two infallible sides.

A pair of Barcelona chairs, palms turned up and empty, sit in the master
bedroom.

Two foolproof, one-hundred proof sides.

Absolut, Bombay, Fortaleza, Glenfiddich, Maker's, Plantation, VSOP, in
   alphabetical order, behind the bar.

Two airtight sides.

A scale the size of a child's fingernail under the slipper tub.

In the chronicles of every horse trade, accord, occupation, agreement,
   massacre, negotiation, bristling apology and unadulterated triumph,

so called.

The wallpaper is Warhol, the ripest figs at the top of the punnet, batteries as
   tall as trees behind the trees in the tropical garden.

How often do the darkest years cast the brightest shadows?

Perfect miniature fixtures adorn the kitchen, in the ballroom glorious
   Lilliputian chandeliers illuminate the walls.

History is lit, history is vanishing.

A lighthouse on the cliff in the landscape

on the foyer wall, a moonless night, a ship making for the rocks

NOTES

Homer. *The Odyssey* with an English Translation by A.T. Murray, Ph.D., in two volumes. Cambridge, MA., Harvard University Press; London, William Heinemann, Ltd. 1919.

[Fagles] asked if it would be acceptable for him to read a passage that bedeviled him. He got up, knelt on the carpet in front of his file cabinet and pulled out some pages. The passage was one of the most famous in "The Aeneid." In Latin it reads, "Forsan et haec olim meminisse iuvabit." "One of the most beautiful lines in Latin," he said, "and also one of the most famous. I know the translation police will be looking, as well as good readers." He peered through his wire rim glasses, and read, "A joy it will be one day, perhaps, to remember even this." He looked at the page for a moment. "It is about loss, about overcoming the worst," he said, "but the word 'perhaps' is important. It may not be a joy to remember. It may be a bloody misery." Hedges, Chris. "PUBLIC LIVES; A Bridge Between the Classics and the Masses." *The New York Times*, April 13, 2004, nytimes.com. 21 June 2023. See also: Marini-Rapoport, Orlee G.S. "Why We Can't Look Back and Laugh." *The Harvard Crimson* 7 April 2020. 21 June 2023. And also: Bostick, Dani. "Forsan et Haec Olim Meminisse Iuvabit: Will Remembering Help or Please?" *In Medias Res* 1 April 2019. 21 June 2023.

"Mỹ Sơn (Vietnamese pronunciation: [miˀ səːn]) is a cluster of abandoned and partially ruined Shaiva Hindu temples in central Vietnam, constructed between the 4th and the 14th century by the Kings of Champa, an Indianized kingdom of the Cham people. The temples are dedicated to the veneration of God in accordance with Shaivism, wherein God is named Shiva, or The Auspicious One. In this particular complex, he is venerated under various local names, the most important of which is Bhadreshvara." "Mỹ Sơn." Wikipedia, The Free Encyclopedia, Wikimedia Foundation, 23 June 2023, en.wikipedia.org/w/index.php?

Acknowledgments

Sincere thanks to Mary Jo Bang for choosing *The Flaws in the Story* for the 2023 Marsh Hawk Poetry Prize, and for your above-and-beyond notes, which made it better.

Many thanks also to the editors of *Colorado Review*, *New Letters*, *Poetry International* and *The Sixty-Four* (Black Mountain Press), in which earlier versions of some of these poems first appeared.

To Sandy McIntosh, Susan Terris and Mark Melnick, bounteous thanks for turning these poems into this beautiful book.

And for all your encouragement, expressed and implicit, and other feedback, love and thanks to and for my family and my family of friends, especially Sonia, Helmut, Harlan, Isaac, Exie, Danielle, Marco, Suzi, Diane, Rosie, Pete, Angela, Heidi and, of course, Jim.

Author Bio

Liane Strauss is the author of *Leaving Eden*, *Frankie, Alfredo,* and *All the Ways You Still Remind Me of the Moon*. She is also the author of the Substack *How To Read a Poem: A Love Story*. She lives in New York City and Guilford, Connecticut.

Titles From Marsh Hawk Press

Jane Augustine *Arbor Vitae; Krazy; Night Lights; A Woman's Guide to Mountain Climbing*
Tom Beckett ~~*Dipstick*~~ *(Diptych)*
William Benton *Light on Water*
Sigman Byrd *Under the Wanderer's Star*
Patricia Carlin: *Original Green; Quantum Jitters; Second Nature*
Claudia Carlson *The Elephant House; My Chocolate Sarcophagus; Pocket Park*
Lorna Dee Cervantes: *April on Olympia*
Meredith Cole *Miniatures*
Jon Curley *Hybrid Moments; Scorch Marks; Remnant Halo*
Joanne D. Dwyer *RASA*
Neil de la Flor *Almost Dorothy; An Elephant's Memory of Blizzards*
Chard deNiord *Sharp Golden Thorn*
Sharon Dolin *Serious Pink*
Joanne Dominique Dwyer *Rasa*
Steve Fellner *Blind Date with Cavafy; The Weary World Rejoices*
Thomas Fink *Zeugma, Selected Poems & Poetic Series; Joyride; Peace Conference; Clarity and Other Poems; After Taxes; Gossip*
Thomas Fink and Maya D. Mason *A Pageant for Every Addiction*
Norman Finkelstein *Inside the Ghost Factory; Passing Over*
Edward Foster *A Looking-Glass for Traytors; The Beginning of Sorrows; Dire Straits; Mahrem: Things Men Should Do for Men; Sewing the Wind; What He Ought to Know*

Paolo Javier *The Feeling is Actual*
Burt Kimmelman *Abandoned Angel; Somehow; Steeple at Sunrise; Zero Point Poiesis; with Fred Caruso The Pond at Cape May Point*
Basil King *Disparate Beasts: Part Two; 77 Beasts; Disparate Beasts; Mirage; The Spoken Word / The Painted Hand from Learning to Draw / A History*
Martha King *Imperfect Fit*
David Lehman *The Birth of* The Best American Poetry
Phillip Lopate *At the End of the Day*
Mary Mackey *Breaking the Fever; The Jaguars That Prowl Our Dreams; Sugar Zone; Travelers With No Ticket Home; Creativity*
Jason McCall *Dear Hero*
Sandy McIntosh *The After-Death History of My Mother; Between Earth and Sky; Cemetery Chess; Ernesta, in the Style of the Flamenco; Forty-Nine Guaranteed Ways to Escape Death; A Hole In the Ocean; Lesser Lights; Obsessional; Plan B:*
Stephen Paul Miller *Any Lie You Tell Will Be the Truth; The Bee Flies in May; Fort Dad; Skinny Eighth Avenue; There's Only One God and You're Not It*
Daniel Morris *Blue Poles; Bryce Passage; Hit Play; If Not for the Courage*
Gail Newman *Blood Memory*
Geoffrey O'Brien *Where Did Poetry Come From; The Blue Hill*
Sharon Olinka *The Good City*
Christina Olivares *No Map of the Earth Includes Stars*
Justin Petropoulos *Eminent Domain*

Paul Pines *Charlotte Songs; Divine Madness; Gathering Sparks; Last Call at the Tin Palace*
Jacquelyn Pope *Watermark*
George Quasha *Things Done for Themselves*
Karin Randolph *Either She Was*
Rochelle Ratner *Balancing Acts; Ben Casey Days; House and Home*
Michael Rerick *In Ways Impossible to Fold*
Corrine Robins *Facing It; One Thousand Years; Today's Menu*
Liane Strauss *The Flaws in the Story*
Eileen R. Tabios *The Inventor: A Poet's Transcolonial Autobiography; Because I Love You I Become War; The Connoisseur of Alleys; I Take Thee, English, for My Beloved; The In(ter)vention of the Hay(na)ku; The Light Sang as It Left Your Eyes; Reproductions of the Empty Flagpole; Sun Stigmata; The Thorn Rosary*
Eileen R. Tabios and j/j hastain *The Relational Elations of Orphaned Algebra*
Tony Trigilio: *Proof Something Happened; Craft: A Memoir*
Susan Terris *Familiar Tense; Ghost of Yesterday; Natural Defenses*
Lynne Thompson *Fretwork*
Madeline Tiger *Birds of Sorrow and Joy*
Tana Jean Welch *Latest Volcano*
Harriet Zinnes: *Drawing on the Wall; Light Light or the Curvature of the Earth; New and Selected Poems; Weather is Whether; Whither Nonstopping*

YEAR	AUTHOR	TITLE	JUDGE
2004	Jacquelyn Pope	*Watermark*	Marie Ponsot
2005	Sigman Byrd	*Under the Wanderer's Star*	Gerald Stern
2006	Steve Fellner	*Blind Date with Cavafy*	Denise Duhamel
2007	Karin Randolph	*Either She Was*	David Shapiro
2008	Michael Rerick	*In Ways Impossible to Fold*	Thylias Moss
2009	Neil de la Flor	*Almost Dorothy*	Forrest Gander
2010	Justin Petropoulos	*Eminent Domain*	Anne Waldman
2011	Meredith Cole	*Miniatures*	Alicia Ostriker
2012	Jason McCall	*Dear Hero,*	Cornelius Eady
2013	Tom Beckett	~~*Dipstick*~~ *(Diptych)*	Charles Bernstein
2014	Christina Olivares	*No Map of the Earth Includes Stars*	Brenda Hillman
2015	Tana Jean Welch	*Latest Volcano*	Stephanie Strickland
2016	Robert Gibb	*After*	Mark Doty
2017	Geoffrey O'Brien	*The Blue Hill*	Meena Alexander
2018	Lynne Thompson	*Fretwork*	Jane Hirshfield
2019	Gail Newman	*Blood Memory*	Marge Piercy
2020	Tony Trigilio	*Proof Something Happened*	Susan Howe
2021	Joanne D. Dwyer	*Rasa*	David Lehman
2022	Brian Cochran	*Translation Zone*	John Yau
2023	Liane Strauss	*The Flaws in the Story*	Mary Jo Bang